The Adventures of

Felix

the Cat

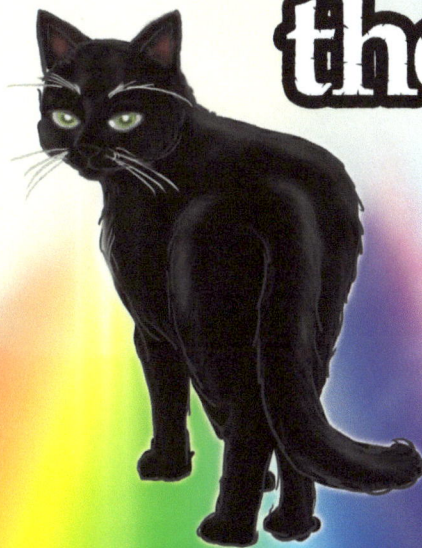

A *Fred Snufflenose* Story

Richard Miller

The Adventures of

Felix
the Cat

A
Fred Snufflenose
Story

Richard Miller

The Adventures of Felix the Cat

Copyright © 2025 by Richard Miller.

This publication contains the opinions and ideas of its author. It is intended to provide helpful and informative material on the subjects addressed in the publication. The author and publisher specifically disclaim all responsibility for any liability, loss, or risk, personal or otherwise, which is incurred as a consequence, directly or indirectly, of the use and application of any of the contents of this book.

MILTON & HUGO L.L.C.
1001 3rd Avenue West,
Suite 430 Bradenton, FL 34205, USA

Website: www. miltonandhugo.com
Hotline: 1- 888-778-0033
Email: info@miltonandhugo.com

Ordering Information:
Quantity sales. Special discounts are available on quantity purchases by corporations, associations, and others. For details, contact the publisher at the address above.

ISBN-13:   979-8-89285-754-3   [Paperback Edition]
              979-8-89285-755-0   [Hardback Edition]
              979-8-89285-753-6   [Digital Edition]

Rev. date: 11/26/2025

Frederick Johann Augustus Snufflenose was sad. No, that doesn't tell enough. He was sadder than sad. His heart was heaving inside his chest, his stomach felt sick and his arms and legs felt like noodles when they are cooked too long. If he had been asked, he would have said he was gi-huge-ick-ly sad, for when Fred Snufflenose was excited or upset, words did not always come out the right way!

Fred and his friend Phil Errup were sitting in a very drab room at the animal health clinic, and Fred was holding his beloved cat, Felix, on his lap. Felix was very calm, which was extremely unusual for him when he was at the clinic. The animal doctor, who is called a veterinarian, was talking to Fred.

However, Fred Snufflenose was having trouble understanding what the doctor was saying…. that's how sad he was.

Felix the cat was old. Fred guessed he was 22 years old, because he had lived with Fred for 20 years, and was already fully grown when he came to live with Fred.

Just that morning, as Fred was getting dressed to go to work, Felix had been curled up into a ball on the bed and had raised his head and given Fred a look so piteous that it had shaken Fred to his very bones. It was as if Felix was saying to Fred, "Won't you please do something to help me? I cannot keep going."

And Fred knew at that moment, that it was time to help Felix to cross the Rainbow Bridge. All day long, Fred had thought about this and the more and more he thought about it, the sadder and sadder he felt.

The vet (which is a lot easier to say than Vet-er-i-nar-i-an), had told Fred that Felix was having something called kidney failure, and although Fred was not a doctor, he knew that was very serious, and he knew what he must do.

Fred was so sad and distressed that he was not aware the Vet had left the room.

"Oh," said Fred, "oh, oh! Where is the doctor?"

"She has gone to get the supplies," answered Phil. "She will be gone for a few minutes. She did ask you if you wanted some time with Felix alone, but you did not answer her, so I told her, "Yes, that would be good."

"I was lost in my sadness," said Fred. Tears were forming in his eyes.

Phil decided it might be a good idea for Fred to think about the funny and crazy adventures that Felix had when he was a young cat.

"Hey, Fred Snufflenose, do you remember when Deborah LaDiva sang the Felix the Cat song to him in German?" And the two of them softly sang to Felix. Felix looked up at them and gave a very quiet and gentle purr.

"Yes, Felix was a real people lover," said Fred. "He was. That is true," said Phil, "I never have known a cat who would run to the door when the bell rang to see who was there. Most cats run in the other direction."

"One Sunday morning," said Fred, "after church, my friend, C. Jane Reade, who works at the book shop, brought her dog Smiley to the apartment for coffee."

"Smiley goes to church and drinks coffee?" asked Phil with surprise.

"No, silly, the coffee was for C. Jane Reade. Her husband was blind and when he was still alive, Smiley was his guide dog. She told me it wouldn't be a problem because Smiley liked cats. I completely forgot that, although Felix loved people, he did not like other animals."

"When I opened my front door, Felix, was right there. He took one look at big old Smiley and turned sideways. His ears went back and his tail got all puffy and huge. He arched his back and his hair stood up. Then, he hissed and he growled. I had never seen him so upset! I closed the door very fast, and that was the end of that adventure."

Fred smiled at the memory. Phil knew his plan was working. Fred was beginning to climb out of his sad state.

"Do you remember me telling you that one night, when I was out of town, Holly Happyhobby was feeding Felix? She forgot to close the windows in my bedroom and a big storm blew up and the wind blew in the corner window and it blew the screen right out of the other window?"

"Yes," said Phil "and Felix went out with the screen. Holly Happyhobby found him two rooftops away."

Fred had lived in a large apartment on the Main Street of the city, way high up. He had to climb 50 steps with the big bags of cat litter and all of the cans of cat food. And besides all those steps, his apartment had two floors, so he had to carry the litter up to the bathroom on the second floor. But he had six gi-huge-ic windows in his bedroom and he could sit at his desk in his very big bedroom and see over the rooftops of most of the buildings in town. It was a fan-tab-u-lous view!

Now, he smiled at the memory. "I always imagined that Felix rode on the window screen as if it were a magic carpet, wearing a turban with a bright red ruby in front of it, and looking very regal."

Phil chuckled at the thought of a small black cat riding on a window screen across the rooftops.

"He was just fine when he was found," said Fred, "and he was also just fine after he fell through the flooring in the great room outside of my apartment."

"Ah, yes," said Phil. "Your friends Paul and Patty Pianissimo were visiting."

"That's right," said Fred, "it was another Sunday morning and we were ready to leave for church. Felix disappeared into a hole in the floor. It dropped way down to a false ceiling for the lower level of the building."

"I was frantic! I didn't know how to get him out. The hole was deeper than my arm was long. Then, Patty sat down and started to play the piano. I asked her, 'Why are you playing the piano when Felix is lost down a hole in the floor?' She told me she thought Felix would think it was me playing and come over to the hole, and so he did! But I still couldn't quite reach him.

"Then my neighbor, Linda Ohnoski came out with some turkey to lure him over to the hole. That brought him running to me. I had to lie down flat on the floor and reach my arm in all the way up to my shoulder and grab him by the scruff of his neck. I was very lucky that I could reach him and he let me do that. Ever since then, I cannot eat turkey lunch meat without Felix wanting some."

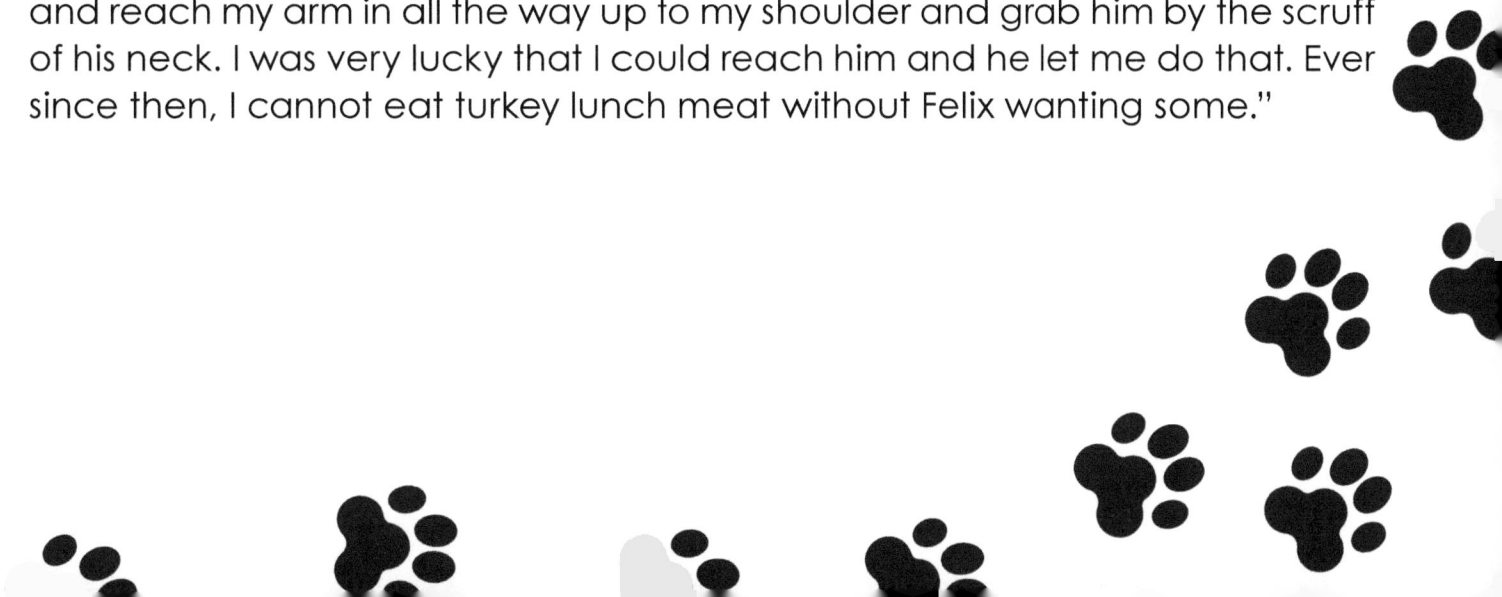

"I also remember when Cathy Greatsinger came to use my piano and began to learn her songs. He would put his ears back and run upstairs! She had a rather large voice."

"And then there was the night he meowed so loudly, it woke me up. Felix had pushed on the screen just enough for something to slip through the opening he made. I looked around the room and saw a large black bug on the wall by my bookcase. Only it wasn't a bug...IT WAS A BAT!!

Felix and I had a race to see who could get out of the bedroom first. I did manage to get the bat out of the window, by knocking it out with a tennis racket. When it was all over, I sat in my favorite chair in the living room, and Felix sat on the window sill next to me, in the dark. He stared and stared up the steps to the second floor. I don't think he believed me when I told him it was okay, the bat was gone."

"After you moved into the apartment in my house on Rimstone Road, when we would watch television together, he used to go to the door at 9:00 p.m. and turn around and stare at me," Phil said.

"Ha, ha, yes, it was time for you to leave!" added Fred. "Then he would go to the steps and stare at me, because he wanted me to come upstairs and pet him as we were getting ready to fall asleep."

Fred sighed, "You really were a wonderful, wonderful cat, Felix, just like the song says," and he gave his sweet kitty a little kiss on the head. "I will never forget you, and I know you will be waiting for me."

Just then the doctor came back, and asked Fred and Phil if they were ready. Fred gulped and then nodded. His eyes brimmed with tears again. The doctor came over to Felix on Fred's lap and gave him the injection, and Felix fell asleep.

Fred told Phil, "Thank you for coming and thank you for reminding me about all the good and fun times Felix had. You are a good friend. And, thank you, Felix," he whispered. "You were a good friend too, and I will always love and remember you."

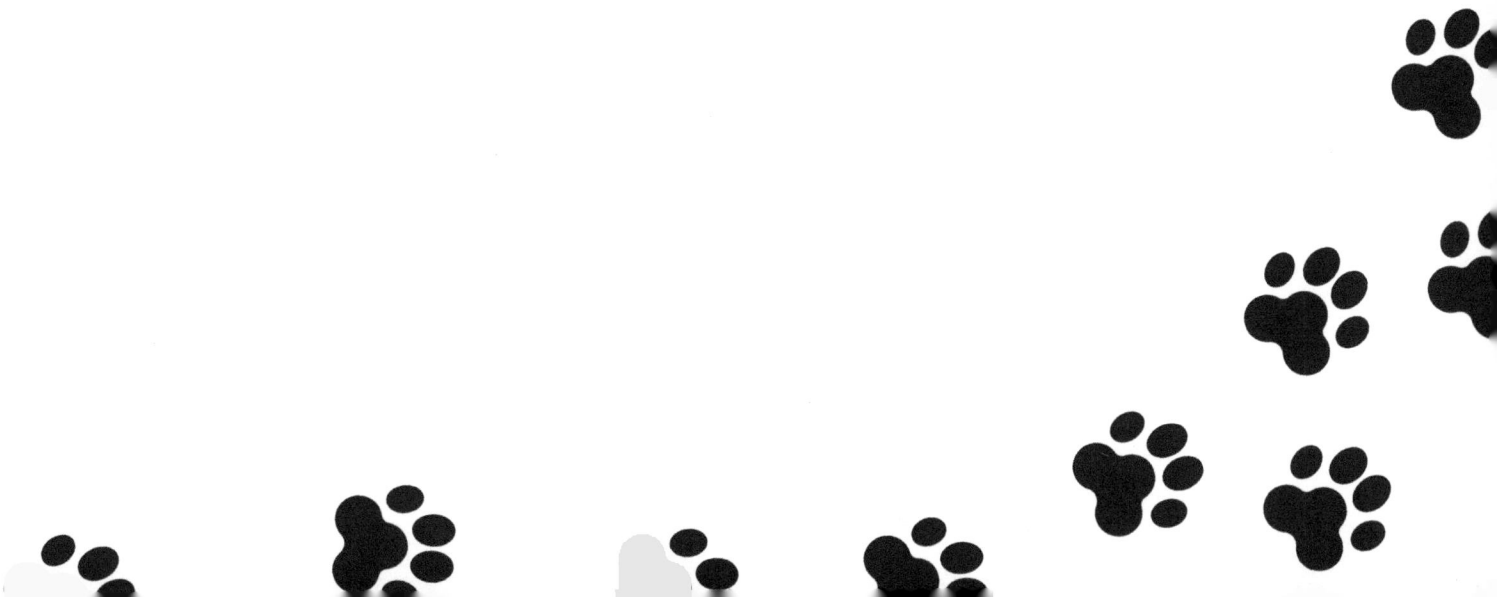

www.ingramcontent.com/pod-product-compliance
Lightning Source LLC
Chambersburg PA
CBHW041559040426
42447CB00002B/233

Fred Snufflenose is dressing for work one morning when his old cat, Felix, looks at him with sad and tired eyes. Fred knows what he must do, but it is not easy for him. In this bittersweet story, Fred and his sidekick, Phil Errup, along with the cat doctor help Felix cross the rainbow bridge. Tears and laughter, and even a song come forth while the two old friends reminisce about Felix's wonderful adventures.

Retired from full time work, Richard Miller resides in Bethlehem, Pennsylvania with his spouse and their four cats. He is the organist in the Old Chapel of Central Moravian Church, where he also leads the Chapel Choir and composes music for them.

MH
MILTON & HUGO

ISBN 979-8-89285-754-3

9798892857543

ANIMALS / CHILDREN

Lord Abernathy Finds A Home

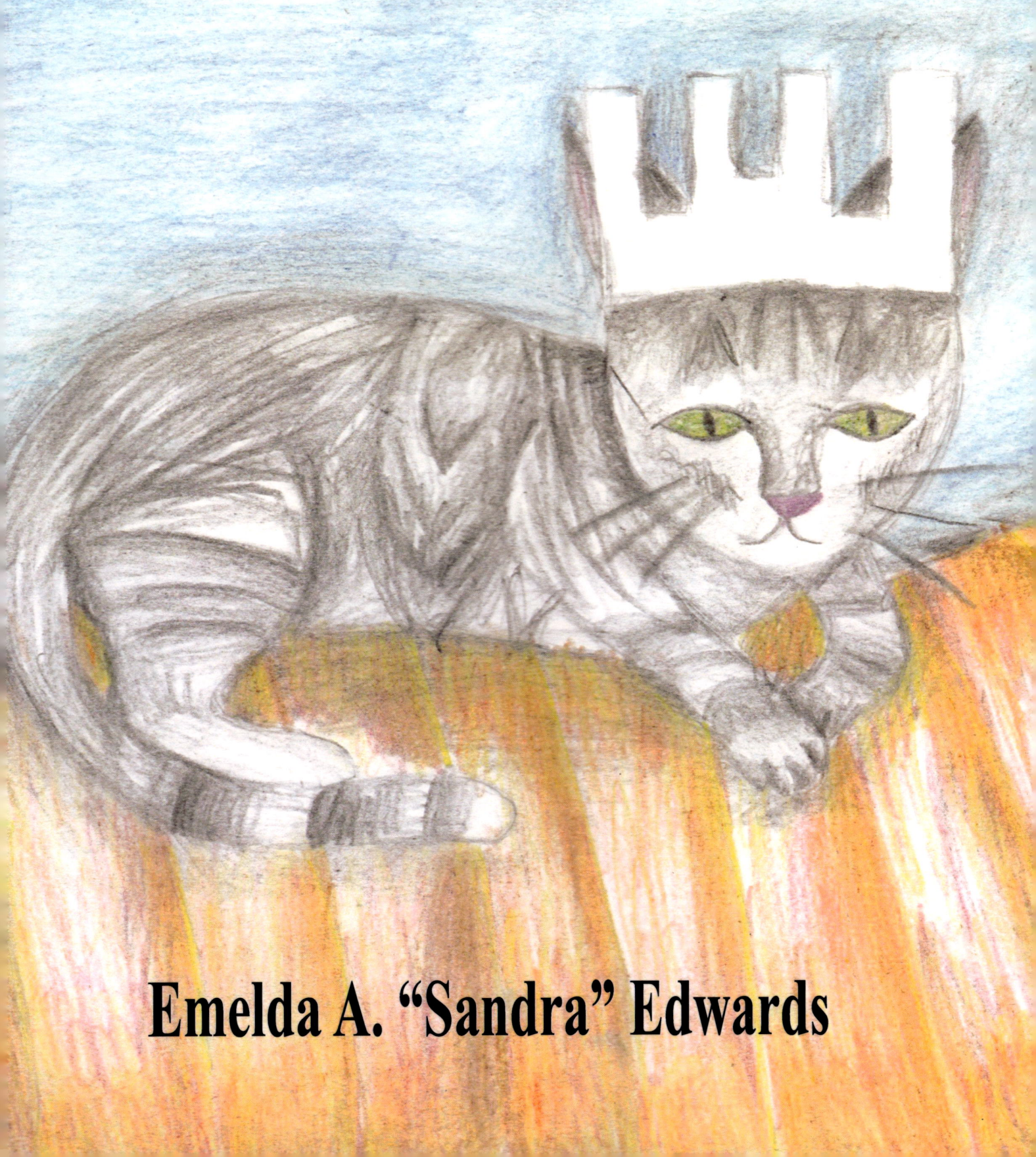

Emelda A. "Sandra" Edwards